Southern

by Jan Norris

Cover photo by Ray Graham, Styling by Jan Norris

Cover design by Ty Walls

(800) 738-3927

Table of Contents

PUDDINGS

COBBLERS

OTHER DELICACIES

Sweet Southern

It wasn't so long ago that dessert was served with every evening meal across America.

Times change; life seems to be moving in a fast lane, even in the South, where the red clay roads are more likely paved today.

Dessert-making has fallen off, giving in to faster meals and slimmer diets.

But in the South, where tradition often holds when all else crumbles, the sweets of long ago can still be found. If not after a nightly meal, then certainly as a centerpiece at a birthday or anniversary.

They're objects of honor, placed with pride at church suppers or family reunion tables.

They're edible hospitality, welcoming newborns, new neighbors and future in-laws. They are the ultimate comfort food, sweet balm for the bitter sting of death at post-funeral gatherings.

From heady whisky-soaked fruitcakes, baked by the half-dozen for holiday gift-giving, to the mighty rich Mississippi mud cake, to the crowd-pleasing red velvet cake, Southern cooks bake up sheer storms when they get started.

Pies are trotted out in rows – far be it from most cooks to settle for just one kind. Pecan, sweet potato, Key lime, the curious chess pie: They're all here, along with cobblers that bubble up beyond their dropped-biscuit crusts and smooth puddings to satisfy that little craving for just a bite of something sweet.

This small book is not meant to be the last word on Southern sweets nor representative of all the South has to offer. That could take volumes.

Instead, it's merely a small sample of tradition, a peek into recipe boxes and stained pages of worn-out cookbooks that chronicle Southern cooking.

Like all recipes, they all have their variations, modifications influenced through the years by family preferences or goods-at-hand. Many are twists on old standards.

The recipes mostly remain true to their roots, however.

We hope you'll enjoy the collection as much as we've enjoyed putting it together.

– Jan Norris

CAKES

APPALACHIAN STACK CAKE

The stack cake was once unique to Appalachia, but today it's found throughout the South. It consists of numerous thin layers of a short "biscuit" cake, layered with dried apples made into a sauce or puree. These are always made in advance; they must "set up" or "ripen" for at least 24 hours.

CAKE
1/2 cup shortening
1 cup brown sugar
1 egg
1 teaspoon vanilla
1/2 cup molasses
1/2 teaspoon baking soda
1 teaspoon baking powder
1/4 teaspoon nutmeg
1/4 teaspoon salt

6 cups flour, plus 1/2 cup
   for rolling dough
1/2 cup buttermilk

DRIED APPLE FILLING
1 cup brown sugar
1 teaspoon cinnamon
1 package (8 ounces) dried
   apples (or peaches)

Make the six-layered cake: Cream shortening and sugar thoroughly in medium bowl of electric mixer. Add egg; beat well. Add vanilla and molasses, beating well.

Sift together baking soda, baking powder, salt, spices and flour in a medium bowl. Add sifted dry ingredients alternately with buttermilk to creamed mixture.

Turn dough out onto a floured surface and let rest about two minutes. Roll dough to about 1/4-inch thickness.

Divide dough into six parts. To portion correctly, roll each ball of dough over the greased bottom of an 8-inch round cake pan. Grease three 8-inch round cake pans and press rolled dough disks into pans.

Bake in 350 degree F oven for 15 minutes. Turn out onto cooling racks to cool. Repeat with remaining dough.

Make the filling: Cook apples (or peaches) according to package directions. Add sugar and cinnamon and cook until combined. Cool.

Stack the cake in layers, adding the apple filling and its juices between each layer. Allow the cake to sit overnight, loosely covered, before cutting; refrigerate after cutting.

Makes six-layer cake.

Note: This cake is best eaten fresh.

APPLESAUCE SPICE CAKE WITH CREAMCHEESE FROSTING

A spice cake is requisite for any baker. This one's made with apple-sauce and has a cream-cheese icing.

1 3/4 cups sugar
1/4 cup packed light brown sugar
1/2 cup (1 stick) butter or margarine
2 eggs
2 1/2 cups all-purpose flour, sifted
2 teaspoons baking powder
1/2 teaspoon baking soda
1 teaspoon cinnamon
1/2 teaspoon nutmeg
1/4 teaspoon allspice

1/4 teaspoon ginger
1 1/2 cups applesauce
1/2 cup raisins
1/2 cup chopped nuts, optional

ICING
1/4 cup butter, softened
8 ounces cream cheese, softened
1 box (1 pound) powdered sugar
1 teaspoon lemon juice

Preheat oven to 325 degrees F. Grease and flour two 9-inch cake pans, or one 13-by-9-inch pan. In a large mixing bowl, beat together sugar, brown sugar and one stick butter.

Beat on medium speed until light and fluffy. Add eggs, one at a time, beating well after each addition.

In a small bowl, combine flour, baking powder, soda and spices. Mix with whisk to combine well. Add flour mixture to batter alternating with applesauce. Beat well after each addition. With rubber spatula, stir in raisins and nuts. Pour batter into prepared baking pan or pans.

Bake for 50 minutes, or until cake springs back to touch in center.

Cool in pans on wire rack for 10 minutes; turn out onto rack to cool completely. (The 13-by-9-inch cake can be frosted in its pan if desired.)

Make icing: Cream together butter and cream cheese in medium bowl of electric mixer. Add sugar gradually, beating in well to combine. Add lemon juice. Continue to beat until smooth. If mixture is too stiff to spread, add milk, a tablespoon at a time, until desired consistency is achieved.

Spread on cooled cake. Sprinkle with chopped nuts if desired.

Makes two 9-inch layers or one 13-by-9-inch cake. This cake freezes very well, even with icing.

BOURBON FRUIT CAKE

Fruitcakes have a long tradition in the South; they're holdovers from Colonial days, brought from Europe. There's much passion on either side of the "light" vs. "dark" cakes; it's simply a matter of preference. It's usually the weekend after Thanksgiving when cooks assemble all the ingredients and bake these cakes. That allows the cakes a month to "set up," a step necessary if cakes are soaked in spirits before being given as Christmas gifts. Rarely do you see a recipe for only one small fruitcake: For all the work involved, even time-pressed cooks from days past felt it was best to make a batch.

2 cups candied mixed fruit
1 cup raisins
1 1/2 cups chopped pecans
3 1/2 cups all-purpose flour
   (divided use)
1 1/2 cups butter, softened
1 cup sugar

6 eggs
1 1/2 teaspoons baking powder
3/4 teaspoon ground nutmeg
1/3 cup milk
1/3 plus 1/2 cup bourbon

Combine candied fruit, raisins, and pecans; dredge in 1/2 cup flour, stirring to coat evenly. Set aside.

Cream butter in a large mixing bowl; gradually add sugar, beating at medium speed with electric mixer until light and fluffy. Add eggs, one at a time, beating well after each.

In a small bowl, using a wire whisk, combine remaining 3 cups flour, baking powder, and nutmeg.

Add flour mixture to creamed mixture alternately with milk, beginning and ending with flour mixture. Do not overbeat. On low speed, stir in 1/3 cup bourbon; add fruit mixture, stirring in by hand with stiff spoon.

Spoon batter into a greased and waxed paper-lined 10-inch tube pan. Bake at 300 degrees F for 1 1/2 hours or until pick interested in center comes out clean. Cool in pan 10 to 15 minutes; remove from pan and cool completely on wire rack; remove paper from bottom of cake.

Moisten several layers of cheesecloth with remaining 1/2 cup bourbon; cover cake completely with cheesecloth.

Put in tin, wrap with aluminum foil and store in cool place at least one week. Remoisten cheesecloth as needed.

BROWN SUGAR POUND CAKE

If there is one cake that symbolizes the South in general, it is the simple Pound Cake. This cake goes to more events and special occasions than almost any other dessert I can name. It gets its name from the pound of each of the main ingredients it used to call for. Here's a popular version.

1 cup butter or margarine, softened
1/2 cup shortening
2 1/4 cups firmly packed brown sugar (approximately 1 pound)
1 cup sugar
5 eggs

3 cups all-purpose flour
1/2 teaspoon baking powder
1/4 teaspoon salt
1 cup milk
2 teaspoons vanilla
1 cup chopped pecans

Preheat oven to 325 degrees F. Grease and flour a 10-inch tube pan.

In a large bowl, cream together butter and shortening. Gradually add brown sugar; beat well to incorporate. Add white sugar and beat until fluffy. Add eggs and beat for two minutes until all is incorporated and mixture is smooth.

Sift together flour, baking powder and salt onto a sheet of waxed paper; pour into medium bowl. Add flour mixture alternately with milk to batter. Add vanilla and beat to incorporate. Stir in nuts by hand.

Pour batter into prepared pan and bake for approximately 1 1/2 hours at 325 degrees. Remove from oven and let stand 10 minutes; turn onto cooling rack and cool completely. Frost as desired.

Makes one 10-inch tube cake.

All pound cakes freeze very well.

BUTTERMILK POUND CAKE

This is the kind of old-fashioned pound cake that shows up at church suppers. It's the best base for fresh strawberries in their syrup. Try it, and you may never again buy those "shortcakes" sold in supermarket produce departments. It freezes very well and is terrific toasted and served with homemade jam.

1 cup butter	1/2 teaspoon salt
3 cups sugar	1/4 teaspoon baking soda
6 eggs	1 cup buttermilk
3 cups flour	1 1/2 teaspoons vanilla extract

Preheat oven to 325 degrees F. Grease and flour a 10-inch tube pan.

In large mixing bowl, cream together butter and sugar until light and fluffy. Add eggs one at a time, beating well after each is added.

On a sheet of waxed paper, sift together flour, salt and baking soda. Add the mixture to the batter alternately with the buttermilk, beating well to incorporate all. Beat in vanilla.

Pour batter into prepared pan and bake at 325 degrees F for 1 1/2 hours. Cake will shrink slightly from side of pan when done.

Makes one 10-inch tube cake.

Coca-Cola® Cake

2 cups flour
2 cups sugar
1 cup (2 sticks) butter
  or margarine
2 tablespoons cocoa
1 cup Coca-Cola®
2 eggs
1 cup buttermilk
1 teaspoon baking soda
2 teaspoons vanilla
1 1/2 cups miniature
  marshmallows

ICING
1/2 cup (1 stick) butter
  or margarine
3 tablespoons unsweetened
  cocoa
1/3 cup Coca-Cola®
1 box (16 ounces) powdered
  sugar
1 cup chopped pecans
  (2 tablespoons reserved)

Grease a 13-by-9-inch baking pan; set aside. Combine flour and sugar in a medium mixing bowl. In a saucepan, heat margarine, cocoa and cola and bring to a boil over medium-high heat. Pour hot mixture over flour and sugar. Set aside.

In a medium mixing bowl, beat eggs until light. Add buttermilk, baking soda, vanilla. Combine with cocoa mixture, mixing well. Stir in marshmallows. Pour batter into prepared pan. Bake at 350 degrees F for 30 to 35 minutes. Be prepared to top with icing when cake is removed from oven.

Make icing: Put butter or margarine, cocoa and cola in a heavy-bottomed saucepan; bring to a boil. Put powdered sugar in medium heat-proof bowl. Pour boiling cocoa mixture over sugar and beat well. Stir in nuts except for reserved 2 tablespoons.

Pour icing over hot cake and spread. Once icing is slightly cool, sprinkle with reserved chopped nuts. Makes one 13-by-9-inch cake. This cake freezes well.

COCONUT CAKE

Coconut lovers simply love this cake. Old-fashioned, gooey and terrific, it's a snowy white beauty sitting high on a milk-glass pedestal. Its other beauty is that it freezes very well.

3 cups cake flour, sifted	**SEVEN-MINUTE FROSTING**
2 teaspoons baking powder	1 cup sugar
1/4 teaspoon salt	1/2 cup corn syrup (light)
1 cup butter	3 tablespoons water
1 pound powdered sugar	3 egg whites
4 egg yolks, well beaten	1/4 teaspoon cream of tartar
1 cup milk	1/4 teaspoon salt
1 teaspoon vanilla	1 1/2 teaspoons vanilla
1 cup shredded coconut	1 1/2 to 2 cups grated coconut
4 egg whites, stiffly beaten	

Grease and flour three 8-inch cake pans or two 9-inch pans (you will split the layers if using two). Preheat oven to 350 degrees F.

On a sheet of waxed paper, sift together flour, baking powder and salt. Sift once more. Set aside.

In a large mixing bowl, beat butter until light and fluffy. Add sugar, a little at a time, and beat well. Add egg yolks, one at a time, beating well after each. Add sifted flour mixture alternately with milk, beating well after each addition. Stir in coconut and vanilla. Fold in egg whites using rubber spatula, taking care to keep batter light.

Divide batter between pans and bake at 350 degrees F for 20 to 30 minutes, depending on pans, or until cakes spring back when lightly touched in centers. Remove and cool in pans five minutes; turn out onto wire rack to cool completely.

Make seven-minute frosting: Combine sugar, corn syrup, water, egg whites, cream of tartar and salt in top of double boiler. (Use mixing bowl, if desired, fitted over saucepan. Do not allow water to touch bottom of pan.)

Cook over rapidly boiling water, beating continuously with electric mixer until mixture stands in peaks. Remove from heat; add vanilla. Continue beating until frosting holds deep swirls.

To assemble cake: Brush crumbs from cake. Spread frosting between layers and sprinkle lightly with coconut. Ice top and sides of cake and press coconut into icing all around sides and on top.

Note: If splitting layers, take care to cut layers evenly. Use toothpicks to mark horizontal center of cake and cut with long knife.

The cake is easier to frost if cut sides are down. Frost as indicated above and cover completely with coconut.

Makes one three-layer 8-inch cake, or one four (split)-one layer 9-inch cake. This cake freezes very well.

COLD OVEN POUND CAKE

This is the old-fashioned plain vanilla pound cake. It's unique in that it begins in a cold oven, hence its name. It's so fast to make, you can bake more than one to have on hand for a "dessert emergency."

1 cup butter or margarine	1 cup heavy cream
1/2 cup shortening	3 cups all-purpose flour
3 cups sugar	1 1/2 teaspoons vanilla extract
3 eggs	(or almond or lemon extract)

Grease and flour a 10-inch tube pan; set aside.

In a large mixing bowl, cream together butter, shortening and sugar. Beat in eggs. Add cream alternately with flour, mixing well after each is added. Beat in extract.

Pour batter in prepared pan and bake at 325 degrees F for 1 1/2 hours. Test with toothpick; it should be clean when inserted in center of cake. Remove and cool in pan for 10 minutes.

Turn out onto wire rack to cool completely.

Makes one 10-inch tube pan. This cake freezes well.

Fresh Fig Cake

A lot of northerners are surprised to find figs growing in the South, but grow they do. Young boys of a certain generation practiced their Red Ryder BB-gun aim on the birds that braved the fire to get to the ripe fruits. Gardeners today use netting to the keep the fruit in and the birds out.

CAKE
2 cups sugar
1/2 cup oil
3 eggs
1 1/2 cups pureed fresh figs
1 teaspoon cinnamon
1 teaspoon nutmeg
1 teaspoon cloves
1 teaspoon soda

Dash (1/8 teaspoon) salt
2 cups flour
1/2 cup milk
1 cup chopped pecans

GLAZE
1 cup brown sugar
1/2 cup milk
1/2 cup margarine

In a large mixing bowl, combine sugar and oil and beat well. Add eggs one at a time. Add figs, spices, soda and salt. Add flour and milk alternately, mixing well. Using a rubber spatula, stir in nuts.

Pour into a greased tube pan or bundt pan. Bake at 350 degrees F for 40 minutes. Lower heat to 325 degrees F and continue baking for 20 minutes more. (Note: The usual tests for cake doneness will not work with this cake.)

Remove cake from oven and pour glaze over cake. Let stand in pan until just warm and remove cake from pan; turn out onto rack.

Make glaze during cake's last 15 minutes in the oven:

Combine brown sugar, milk and margarine in saucepan. Bring to a boil over medium-high heat and simmer for three minutes; remove and cool slightly.

When ready to glaze, place cake on rimmed cake plate. Pour glaze slowly over cake, allowing it to drip down sides and center. Makes one tube or bundt cake. This cake freezes well, but note that it takes two hours to completely thaw. It is best served warm or at room temperature.

Fresh Orange Cake

Oranges are always abundant on backyard trees in South Florida beginning in fall, and at the holidays, this cake makes its special appearance.

3 yellow cake layers
(use the 1-2-3-4 cake recipe
on page 44 if desired)
8 thin-skinned "juice" oranges

1 small can frozen orange juice
concentrate, thawed but
chilled
2 cups sugar

Bake cake and allow to cool completely. Wash oranges well and dry. Grate the peel only from all oranges on the fine teeth of a box grater. Juice oranges, straining out seeds. Put grated peel and juice in a medium bowl. Add thawed orange juice concentrate. Add sugar and stir well to completely dissolve.

Let stand 30 minutes in refrigerator. The syrup should be slightly thickened. If it is too thin, add 1/4 cup more sugar, stir and let stand again. Divide syrup into two bowls. One bowl is for the bottom two layers, while the second bowl is for the top and sides.

Assemble cake:

Note: Use a cake plate with a lip on it as the syrup may run.

Place 1 layer on the plate and spoon a few tablespoons of syrup over cake. Use a bamboo skewer to make small holes in cake surface for liquid to run through.

When syrup is absorbed add more, drizzling sides. Repeat with second layer and syrup, using up all the syrup in the first bowl for the bottom two layers. Repeat with top layer, using second bowl of syrup.

Note: Adding the syrup is a two- or three-hour procedure and should be done slowly, allowing the cake to absorb the liquid before adding more. Spoon up any syrup that pools on the cake plate and pour it back over the layers.

Makes one three-layer cake. Once completed, the cake must be refrigerated. It freezes very well and is best served cold.

HOT MILK CAKE

This traditional cake is often used as a yellow-cake base. It freezes well and is nice for a quick small birthday cake.

3/4 cup milk	**1 1/2 cups all-purpose flour**
1/4 cup butter	**2 teaspoons baking powder**
3 eggs, well beaten	**1 teaspoon vanilla extract**
1 1/2 cups sugar	

Preheat oven to 350 degrees F. In a small saucepan, combine milk and butter. Heat over medium-low burner until butter is melted; remove.

In a mixing bowl, beat eggs until lemon-color. Add sugar, a little at a time, until well incorporated. Onto a sheet of waxed paper, sift together flour with baking powder.

With mixer on medium, add flour and milk alternately to egg mixture, beating well after each addition. Add vanilla.

Bake in two 8-inch layer pans at 350 degrees for 20 minutes, or until cake springs back when touched lightly. Frost as desired.

Makes two 8-inch layers.

HUMMINGBIRD CAKE

*There's no official record of the origin of this cake that I have found,
but it could have come from the mad rush to create something with
canned pineapple in the '50s, when Hawaii became a state.
Its tropical nature makes this a favorite along the Gulf Coast
and in South Florida, where bananas grow in back yards.
It's another church-supper staple.*

CAKE
3 cups all-purpose flour
2 cups sugar
1 teaspoon baking soda
1 teaspoon salt
1 teaspoon ground cinnamon
3 eggs, beaten
1 cup chopped bananas
1 cup vegetable oil
1 1/2 teaspoons vanilla extract
1 can (8 ounces) crushed
    pineapple in syrup

1 cup pecans, chopped

FROSTING
1 large package (8 ounces)
    cream cheese, softened
1/2 cup margarine, softened
1 box (16 ounces) powdered
    sugar, sifted
1 teaspoon vanilla
1/2 cup pecans, chopped

Preheat oven to 350 degrees F. Grease and flour three 9-inch
round cake pans. Set aside.

In a large bowl, combine flour, sugar, soda, salt and cinnamon. With rubber spatula, stir in eggs and oil, stirring until
flour mixture is just moistened. (Note: Do not use mixer.) Stir
in vanilla, pineapple with its syrup, pecans, and bananas.

Bake at 350 degrees for 25 to 30 minutes, or until a wooden
toothpick inserted in center comes out clean. Cool in pans 10
minutes.

Turn out onto cooling racks and cool completely.

Make frosting: Combine cream cheese and margarine, beating until smooth. Add powdered sugar; beat until light and fluffy. Beat in vanilla. Spread between layers and on top and sides of cake. Sprinkle pecans on top. Makes one 3-layer cake.

Note: Store in refrigerator; this cake also freezes well.

KENTUCKY JAM CAKE

The jam cake is found among Southern recipes in Tennessee and Kentucky writings. Many recipes migrated between these two states, just as residents did. Often, certain fruits are spelled out for the jam, with blackberry and plum being two favorites. Use a commercial version that has mostly fruit for today's baking if you don't have homemade jam on hand.

1 cup butter or shortening (or a mix of the two)	5 tablespoons sour cream or sour milk
1 cup sugar	1 cup jam
1 teaspoon baking soda	
3 1/2 cups flour	
1/2 teaspoon allspice	For topping: 2 cups jam, melted over low heat
1/2 teaspoon cloves	

Grease and flour two 9-inch round cake pans.

Preheat oven to 350 degrees F. In a mixing bowl on medium speed, combine butter and sugar until fluffy. Sift together the soda, flour and spices. Add the flour mixture alternately with the sour cream or milk, beating well after each addition. Stir in jam.

Divide batter between two prepared pans, and rap on counter

to release any air bubbles. Bake at 350 degrees until tops of cakes in center spring back at touch; 20 to 25 minutes.

Cool cakes on racks for 10 minutes, then turn out on racks to cool completely. When completely cool, divide melted jam and spread half between the layers, and half on top of cake. Makes one 9-inch cake.

Note: This cake freezes well. Wrap cake in plastic wrap, then in foil and freeze. Thaw for one hour before serving; it's very good when cold.

LADY BALTIMORE CAKE

In Maryland, you may be treated to the Lady Baltimore Cake, a special white cake filled with fruits and nuts but bearing no resemblance to a fruitcake.

1 cup butter, softened
1 3/4 cups white sugar
1 1/2 teaspoons vanilla extract
3 cups all-purpose flour
1 tablespoon baking powder
1/2 teaspoon salt
1 cup milk
6 egg whites

FILLING
2 cups sugar
1/2 cup water
1/4 cup corn syrup

Dash salt
4 egg whites
1/4 teaspoon cream of tartar
1 teaspoon vanilla extract
  (or cognac)
1/2 cup raisins, coarsely
  chopped
1/2 cup chopped pecans,
  toasted
1/3 cup chopped candied
  cherries
2 teaspoons cognac or sherry

Preheat oven to 350 degrees F. Grease and flour three 9-inch cake pans.

23

In a large mixing bowl, cream together butter, 1 1/4 cups sugar and vanilla. Beat well.

Onto a sheet of waxed paper, sift together flour, baking powder and salt. Add flour mixture to butter mixture, alternating with milk. Beat well after each addition.

In a large bowl, beat egg whites until stiff. Add 1/2 cup sugar and beat until dissolved; egg whites should not be dry. Fold egg whites into batter using rubber spatula. Divide batter among the prepared pans.

Bake at 350 degrees F for 25 to 30 minutes, or until cake springs back when lightly touched in center. Remove and cool in pans five minutes; loosen and turn out onto wire racks to cool completely.

Make frosting: In medium heavy-bottomed saucepan over medium-high heat, stir together sugar, water, corn syrup and salt.

Cook, without stirring, for approximately seven minutes to a soft-ball stage (240 degrees F on candy thermometer). A drop of the syrup in ice water will form a soft ball, and a thin thread will hang from the spoon.

In a medium heatproof bowl, beat egg whites with cream of tartar to form stiff peaks.

When syrup is ready, pour it slowly into the egg whites, with mixer running continuously. A creamy meringue is the result.

Add vanilla or cognac for flavoring. Allow mixture to cool.

In small bowl, mix together raisins, nuts and cherries and sprinkle with cognac or sherry. Let stand until meringue is cooled.

Once cooled, mix together meringue, fruits and nuts. Spread between layers and onto of cake.

Makes one 3-layer cake. This cake is best eaten fresh.

LANE CAKE

This cake was my mother's pride and joy at Christmas. It sat, like the jewel that it is, on the counter on a milk-glass pedestal cake stand. Guests were reluctant to cut into it, but never backed down when offered a piece. I only recently learned that the cake was a top prize winner for its creator, Emma Rylander Lane, at the Alabama State Fair years ago. A heavy hand with bourbon in the icing may tilt judges in your favor, too.

CAKE

1 cup (2 sticks) butter or
  margarine, softened
2 cups sugar
3 1/4 cups flour
1 teaspoon baking powder
3/4 teaspoon salt
1 cup milk
1 teaspoon vanilla extract
8 egg whites, stiffly beaten

FILLING AND ICING

12 egg yolks
2 1/4 cups sugar
3/4 cup butter or margarine
1 1/2 cups chopped pecans
1 1/2 cups raisins
1 1/2 cups flaked coconut
1/3 to 3/4 cup bourbon
3/4 cup chopped maraschino
  cherries

Preheat oven to 325 degrees F. Grease and flour three 9-inch round cake pans. Line bottoms with waxed paper and grease again. Set aside.

Cream butter in large mixing bowl until light and fluffy. Add sugar, beating well to incorporate.

Sift together flour, baking powder and salt onto a sheet of waxed paper; pour into a medium bowl. Add the flour mixture alternately with milk to the creamed mixture, beating well after each addition. Stir in vanilla.

Beat egg whites in medium bowl until stiff. Fold into batter.

Divide batter evenly between the three pans.

Bake at 325 degrees F for 25 minutes or until a wooden pick inserted in the center of a cake comes out clean. Cool in pans 10 minutes. Turn out onto racks and remove paper from cakes; cool completely before frosting.

Make frosting: Combine egg yolks, sugar and butter in a 2-quart heavy-bottomed saucepan.

Cook over medium heat, stirring constantly, about 20 minutes, until thickened. Remove from heat and stir in remaining ingredients. Cool completely before using.

Assemble: Place one cake layer on serving plate; put frosting on top.

Repeat with second layer, frosting top and sides for both layers.

Top with remaining layer and frost top and remaining sides of cake.

Makes one 3-layer cake.

This cake freezes very well and becomes better the longer it sits. Leftovers should be refrigerated.

LAZY DAISY CAKE

While this cake shows up in Southern recipe boxes everywhere, it also appears in several other cookbooks from around the country. As with so many other cakes, its origins are sketchy.

1 1/2 cups flour	5 tablespoons butter, melted
1/2 teaspoon salt	1 cup water
1 teaspoon baking soda	
1 cup sugar	ICING
3 1/2 tablespoons unsweetened cocoa	3 egg whites
	1/2 cup brown sugar
1 teaspoon vanilla	1 teaspoon vanilla
1 tablespoon vinegar	Chopped nuts for garnish

Preheat oven to 350 degrees F. Set eggs for icing on counter to bring to room temperature. Grease a 9-inch square pan; set aside.

Over a sheet of waxed paper, sift together flour, salt, soda, sugar and cocoa powder. Pour mixture into a medium mixing bowl.

Use the back of a spoon to make three indentations in the mixture. Into one pour vanilla. Into another, add vinegar, and into the third, the melted butter. Pour water over all, and mix well until smooth. Pour batter into prepared pan and bake 30 minutes or until finger leaves depression in top of cake.

Meanwhile, make icing, which will be added to cake before it is completely done.

Beat egg whites until stiff. Slowly add brown sugar, beating well. Add vanilla and beat with rubber spatula; mixture should be a stiff meringue.

Spread icing on cake for last seven minutes of baking. Sprinkle chopped nuts on top if desired, to toast at the same time.

Bake for five to seven minutes, watching so icing does not overbrown. Remove to rack to cool in pan.

Makes 1 9-inch square cake. This cake is best eaten the same day; the toasted meringue does not freeze well.

LEMON POUND CAKE

The lemon pound cake is a summertime treat. Iced with fresh lemon glaze, it's great with spiced tea.

6 tablespoons butter	1 teaspoon lemon juice
2/3 cup granulated sugar	1/2 teaspoon vanilla extract
4 egg yolks	1/2 teaspoon lemon extract
1 1/4 cups cake flour	
1 1/2 teaspoons baking powder	**GLAZE**
1/8 teaspoon salt	Juice of 1 lemon
1/3 cup milk	Grated peel of 1 lemon
2 teaspoons finely grated	1 1/2 cups powdered sugar
lemon peel	1 tablespoon milk (or as need)

Preheat oven to 325 degrees F. Grease well and flour a standard (5-by-9-by-3-inch) loaf pan.

In a mixing bowl, cream the butter with sugar until light and fluffy. In a separate bowl, beat the egg yolks until light. Beat yolks into creamed butter.

On a sheet of waxed paper, sift together the flour, baking powder and salt. Gradually add flour mixture to the first mixture, alternating with the milk. Beat well. Add lemon peel and juice and the extracts, beating well to incorporate.

28

Pour batter into a well-greased and floured 5-by-9-by-3-inch loaf pan. Bake until a wooden pick inserted into the center comes out clean and the cake pulls away from the sides of the pan, about 45 to 50 minutes. Cool in pan on rack for about 45 minutes; remove from pan and cool thoroughly.

Make the glaze: Combine all ingredients in small cup. Stir well to make a smooth glaze. Drizzle with spoon over cooled cake.

Makes one 9-inch loaf. This cake freezes very well.

"LIGHT" FRUITCAKE

pound candied cherries	1 pound (3 1/2 cups)
pound candied pineapple	all-purpose flour
pound pecans	1 teaspoon baking powder
pound butter or margarine, softened	1/4 teaspoon salt
pound confectioners' sugar	3 tablespoons vanilla extract
eggs, separated	1/3 cup brandy or other spirit
	1/2 cup orange juice

Grease and flour two 8-inch tube pans. Line the bottoms with waxed paper and grease tops of waxed paper. Set aside.

Dice fruits and lightly toss with flour to coat. Chop nuts and add to fruits. Set fruits and nuts aside.

In a large mixing bowl, cream together butter and sugar until light and fluffy. Add egg yolks, one at a time, and blend well. Sift together flour, baking powder and salt. Add floured fruits and nuts.

Mix vanilla, brandy and orange juice in a small bowl. Com-

29

bine flour and fruit mixture with butter mixture, alternately adding vanilla-orange juice mixture.

In a medium bowl, beat egg whites until stiff but not dry. Fold into batter. Divide batter evenly between the two prepared pans.

Bake slowly over a pan of hot water placed in oven bottom at 275 degrees F for two hours or until straw or pick inserted in center comes out clean.

Cool in pans for 30 minutes; turn out onto cake rack to dry completely (peel off paper).

To keep: Wrap well in cheesecloth soaked in brandy. Place in air-tight container or tin and soak cloth every two weeks for up to a month with a sprinkle of brandy.

This cake can be frozen, but it's best eaten when completely thawed. Makes two 8-inch round fruitcakes.

MISSISSIPPI MUD CAKE

*No one is quite sure where this cake got started, but it hit like wildfire
in the '60s and early '70s. It's now a staple at church suppers, bake
sales and any occasion that's right for cake.*

CAKE
1 stick butter
1/2 cup cocoa
5 eggs (use extra large, or
   substitute 6 large eggs)
1 1/4 cups sifted self-rising
   flour
2 cups white sugar
1 cup (or more as desired)
   chopped nuts

2 teaspoons vanilla
TOPPING
1 bag miniature marshmallows
1 box powdered sugar
1/2 cup (1 stick) butter,
   softened
1/3 cup unsweetened cocoa
   powder
1/2 cup evaporated milk
Chopped nuts, optional

Melt butter; add cocoa, eggs, sugar, and flour; mix well. Stir
in nuts and vanilla, then pour into a greased 13-by-9-inch sheet
cake pan.

Bake at 350 degrees F for 30 minutes or until top of cake
barely springs back when touched. (This cake is best under-
baked.) Be ready to frost the cake immediately after baking.

While cake is baking, make topping:

In a medium bowl, beat together the sugar and butter. Sift
in cocoa and beat again. Add milk and beat until smooth and
creamy.

Cover the top of the cake with marshmallows immediately
as you take it out of oven. Pour the frosting over the marshmallows before they melt, and swirl together on top of cake.
Sprinkle with chopped nuts, if desired. Cool briefly before
cutting.

Makes one 13-by-9-inch sheet cake.

MORAVIAN SUGAR CAKE

North Carolina is well-known for the Moravian churches that dot the area; the church sales and several bakeries feature this unusual cake with European origins as a holiday cake or breakfast cake.

1 package dry yeast
1/2 cup warm water
1 cup hot mashed potatoes
 (with no seasonings)
1 cup sugar
1/2 cup shortening
1/4 cup butter, softened
1 teaspoon salt

2 eggs, beaten
5 to 6 cups (as needed)
 all-purpose flour

TOPPING
Brown sugar
Butter, melted
Cinnamon

Peel, boil and mash potatoes; have ready, warmed. Grease two jelly-roll pans or two 13-by-9-inch baking pans. Set aside.

Sprinkle yeast over warm (115-degree F) water.

In a large mixing bowl, mix mashed potatoes, sugar, shortening, butter and salt. Add yeast mixture and stir well. (This mixture is called the sponge.) Cover the bowl and let sit in a warm place until it has risen and is spongelike.

With stiff spoon, beat in eggs. Add flour until dough becomes soft and holds together in a ball. Form into a ball and place in a greased bowl, flip dough to coat with grease, cover with a towel. Set in a warm place and let rise until doubled in size, about two hours.

Turn dough onto floured workspace and knead well, about five minutes, or until dough is smooth and elastic. Divide dough in two. Press dough gently onto each of the two prepared baking pans. Set in a warm place to rise again until doubled, about 20 minutes.

32

When dough is ready to bake, make indentations in the dough every 2 inches apart with fingers, and fill with brown and melted butter. Sprinkle cinnamon over all.

Bake at 375 degrees F for approximately 20 minutes or until golden brown. Remove and cool before wrapping tightly to keep or freeze.

Makes two 13-by-9-inch cakes.

NEW ORLEANS KING CAKE

By now, everyone's familiar with the New Orleans Mardi Gras party tradition, the King Cake. It's similar in texture to the Moravian Sugar Cake and also is made with yeast. A tiny baby doll or dried bean is baked into the cake. The person who is served the baby is crowned king and must bake the cake for the next party.

1/4 cup butter
2 cups (16 ounces) sour cream
1/3 cup sugar
1 teaspoon salt
2 envelopes dry yeast
1 tablespoon sugar
1/2 cup warm water
2 eggs
6 to 6 1/2 cups flour, sifted
1/2 cup sugar
1 1/2 teaspoons cinnamon
1/3 cup butter

COLORED SUGARS
yellow, green and purple food
 coloring pastes
3/4 cup white sugar

ICING
3 cups confectioners' sugar
1/4 cup lemon juice
3 to 6 tablespoons water
1 plastic baby or dried red bean

Combine butter, sour cream, sugar and salt in a medium saucepan. Heat over medium-low till butter melts, stirring. Remove and cool slightly.

In large bowl dissolve yeast and 1 tablespoon sugar in warm (115-degree F) water. Let stand five minutes.

Add the cool butter mixture, beaten eggs and 2 cups of flour. Beat at medium speed for two minutes or till smooth. Gradually stir in enough remaining flour to make soft dough.

Turn dough onto a lightly floured workspace and knead until smooth and elastic, about seven minutes. Place in a well-greased bowl, flip dough to coat with grease and cover with a damp towel. Let rise in warm place until doubled in bulk.

Combine 1/2 cup of sugar and cinnamon; set aside.

Punch air from dough, knead briefly and divide in half. Turn one part of dough onto floured surface and roll into a 28-by-10-inch rectangle. Spread half of the butter and cinnamon-sugar mixture on dough. Roll dough, jelly-roll fashion, and set aside (insert baby doll or bean at this time if using). Repeat with remaining dough.

Place the rolls, seams down, on a well-greased baking sheet in the form of a crescent. Bring roll ends together to form an oval ring. Cover and let rise in warm place 20 minutes or until doubled in size.

Bake at 375 F for 15 to 20 minutes or until light golden. Remove and cool slightly before adding icing.

Make colored sugars: Use the back of a spoon to rub each colored paste separately into a bowl of 1/4 cup sugar.

Make icing: Combine sugar, lemon juice and 3 tablespoons water in small cup; mix until smooth. Add more water, if needed, to make icing fluid.

Spread icing over top of cake. Immediately sprinkle the

colored sugars in patches or in a pattern over the cake – do not mix the colors, as you should see yellow, green and purple, the colors of Mardi Gras.

Makes one King Cake, enough to serve 12 to 16.

OLD-FASHIONED JAM CAKE

The following version of the jam cake is credited to the Martha White Flour company.

CAKE
1 cup sugar
1/2 cup butter or margarine
1/2 teaspoon vanilla extract
3 eggs
1 1/2 cups all-purpose flour
1/2 teaspoon baking soda
1/2 teaspoon allspice
1/2 teaspoon cinnamon
1/2 teaspoon cloves
1/4 teaspoon salt
1/2 cup buttermilk (see note)

1 cup blackberry jam
1/2 cup strawberry preserves
1/2 cup raisins
1/2 cup chopped walnuts

GLAZE
1/4 cup butter or margarine
1/2 cup firmly packed dark
   brown sugar
1/4 cup milk
1 teaspoon vanilla
2 cups powdered sugar

Heat oven to 325 degrees F. Grease bottoms of two 8-inch cake pans. Line pans with greased and floured waxed or parchment paper. Grease and flour sides of pans.

In large bowl, combine sugar and ´ cup butter; beat until light and fluffy. Add vanilla; blend well. Add eggs individually, beating well after each is added.

35

In a small bowl, stir flour with baking soda, spices and salt, using wire whisk. Add to egg mixture alternately with buttermilk. Add jam and preserves to cake mixture. Beat two minutes at medium speed. Stir in raisins and walnuts.

Pour batter into greased and floured pans. Bake at 325 degrees F for 45 to 50 minutes or until toothpick inserted in center comes out clean. Cool 10 minutes and turn out onto cooling rack. Cool completely.

Make glaze: Heat butter, brown sugar and milk in a saucepan over medium low heat until combined and sugar is completely melted. Bring to a boil, stirring constantly. Remove from heat and stir in vanilla. Beat in sugar until glaze is smooth.

To assemble: Place one layer on serving plate. Spread about 1/3 of the warm glaze over the first layer. Top with second layer and repeat, allowing glaze to drip down sides. Store refrigerated.

Cake freezes well. Makes two 8-inch layers.

PINEAPPLE UPSIDE-DOWN CAKE

There's not a baker around, North or South, who doesn't have an up-side-down cake in his or her repertoire. In the South, it's the "other" use for the cast iron skillet, cornbread being first and foremost. If you must use a mix to substitute for the cake batter, use a one-layer cake or half a package of a regular boxed mix.

UPSIDE-DOWN TOPPING
2 tablespoons butter
1 cup light brown sugar
1 can pineapple rings (use syrup in cake, if desired)
1/2 cup chopped pecans (optional)
Whole maraschino cherries (optional)

CAKE
1 1/2 cups flour
2 1/2 teaspoons baking powder
1/4 teaspoon salt
1/2 cup sugar
1/2 cup milk
1 egg
1 teaspoon vanilla extract
3 tablespoons butter or shortening, melted

A 10-inch iron skillet is needed for this recipe. Preheat oven to 350 degrees F.

While oven heats, put butter in skillet and set in oven to melt; remove when just melted. Add brown sugar and stir. Arrange pineapple rings in skillet, sides touching. Cut up a ring to fill in spaces as needed. Put nuts in between rings and cherries, if used, in center of rings. Set aside.

Make the cake: sift together flour, baking powder and salt. Beat sugar, milk and egg and reserved pineapple juice together until combined. Add vanilla and melted butter; mix well. Combine with flour mixture, mixing well.

Pour batter into skillet over prepared pineapple rings. Bake at 350 degrees F until cake springs back in center when lightly touched.

Remove skillet from oven and invert onto 12-inch serving plate. Leave skillet on top of cake for two minutes or until all sugars have had time to melt onto sides. Carefully remove skillet.

Chill cake as desired. Makes one single-layer 10-inch cake. This cake will freeze, but it's best eaten fresh.

Note: Peach or apple slices can be substituted for pineapple, but add 1/2 cup water or milk to batter to substitute for missing pineapple liquid.

RED VELVET CAKE

This is one of the South's more intriguing cakes, materializing at all occasions, especially Christmas and Valentine's Day, as well as at some weddings under the guise of "groom's cake." It won a cameo role in the movie, Steel Magnolias, *taking the form of an armadillo whose crimson innards are revealed when sliced.*

CAKE
2 1/4 cups all-purpose flour, sifted
1 teaspoon salt
2 tablespoons cocoa
1 1/2 ounces red food coloring
1/2 cup shortening or vegetable oil
1 1/2 cups sugar
2 eggs
1 cup buttermilk
1 teaspoon vanilla
1 tablespoon vinegar

1 teaspoon baking soda

CREAM CHEESE ICING
1/4 cup (1/2 stick) butter
8 ounces cream cheese, room temperature
1 pound box of powdered sugar
Dash of salt
1/2 teaspoon vanilla
1 cup chopped pecans, toasted

Preheat oven to 350 degrees F. Grease and flour three 8-inch cake pans. (Or you can use two 9-inch pans and split the layers into four.) Sift together flour and salt; set aside.

In a small glass measuring cup, mix together the cocoa and food coloring, stirring until smooth and cocoa is dissolved. (This ensures an even coloring throughout the cake.)

In a large mixing bowl, cream together the shortening and sugar, beating for four minutes at medium speed or until fluffy. Add the eggs, one at a time, beating for at least 30 seconds after each addition. (Do not underbeat at this stage.) To the egg mixture, with mixer on low, alternately add the flour mixture, the buttermilk and vanilla. Scrape down sides and beat again to incorporate. Add the cocoa/food coloring mixture, beating until color of batter is uniform. Do not overbeat at this stage, or cake will be tough.

In a small bowl, stir together the vinegar and baking soda. (Note: It will foam up.) Stir it briefly to mix, and then add it to the cake batter with a rubber spatula (do not beat it in), folding it in to incorporate well.

Pour the batter into the prepared cake pans, and bake in a 350-degree F oven for 25 to 30 minutes, or until a cake tester comes out clean. Allow layers to cool on a rack for 10 minutes before turning out. Let cake cool completely before frosting.

Make frosting: In a medium mixing bowl, beat together butter and cream cheese; gradually beat in powdered sugar and salt, scraping sides frequently. On low speed, beat in vanilla.

To frost cake, chill cake layers well first (this prevents crumbs from getting into icing). Spread a thin layer between cake layers, and use bulk of icing for sides and top. Top cake with chopped nuts, or if desired, press them into sides of cake, making a 3-inch "rim" around bottom. This cake freezes well.

SAM HOUSTON'S WHITE CAKE

This is another cake whose origins are unknown, though Sam Houston is said to have been fond of it. Houston was governor of two states (Tennessee and Texas) and the man who won Texas from Mexico. The cake is a white with chocolate frosting. To provide extra white contrast, go to a cake-decorating store to find clear vanilla extract.

CAKE
3/4 cup butter, softened
2 cups sugar
3 cups all-purpose flour
1 tablespoon baking powder
1/2 teaspoon salt
1/2 cup milk
1/2 cup water
1/2 teaspoon almond extract
1 teaspoon vanilla extract
6 egg whites, at room temperature

CHOCOLATE FROSTING
3 (1-ounce) squares unsweetened chocolate
4 cups sifted powdered sugar
1/8 teaspoon salt
1/4 cup hot water
3 egg yolks
1/4 cup butter or margarine, melted
1 teaspoon vanilla extract

Grease and flour three 9-inch cake pans. Set aside. Preheat oven to 350 degrees F.

In a large mixing bowl using an electric mixer, cream butter on medium speed. Gradually add sugar and beat well.

In a medium bowl, combine flour, baking powder, and salt with wire whisk.

In another small bowl, stir together milk and water. Add flour mixture to creamed mixture alternately with milk mixture, beginning and ending with flour mixture. Mix well after each addition. Stir in extracts.

In a medium bowl, using a whisk or the electric mixer, beat egg whites until stiff peaks form. Use a rubber spatula to fold whites into batter. Pour batter into three greased and floured 9-inch round cake pans.

Bake at 350 degrees for 25 minutes or until a wooden pick inserted in the center comes out clean. Cool in pans for 10 minutes; turn out onto wire rack and allow to cool completely.

Make frosting: Put chocolate in top of a double boiler and place over gently simmering water. Cook until melted.

Remove from heat and add sugar, salt and hot water. Beat with electric mixer until mixture is thoroughly blended. Add egg yolks, one at a time, beating after each addition. Add butter and vanilla and beat until frosting reaches spreading consistency.

Spread on top and sides of cake.

Makes one three-layer, 9-inch cake. This cake freezes very well.

7-UP® CAKE

Using a soft drink in a cake is just something Southerners do. In Georgia's neck of the woods, it's Coca-Cola® (SEE RECIPE ON PAGE 14). The 7-Up® Cake is unique for its use of a boxed mix and a pudding mix to boot. You can use a carbonated beverage of your choice.

1 box yellow cake mix
4 eggs
1 small box pineapple or
    vanilla pudding (not instant)
3/4 cup oil
1 bottle (10 ounces) 7-Up®
    soft drink

ICING
2 eggs, beaten
1 1/2 cups sugar
1 rounded tablespoon flour
1/2 cup (1 stick) butter or
    margarine, melted
1 small can crushed pineapple
1/2 cup toasted pecans (optional)
1 1/2 cups coconut

In bowl of an electric mixer, combine cake mix, eggs, pudding and oil; mix well. Beat until light and fluffy – about 4 minutes at medium-high speed. Lower mixer speed to slow and gradually beat in soft drink. Mix well.

Pour batter into 13-by-9-inch greased baking pan. Bake at 325 degrees F for 40 to 45 minutes.

While cake bakes, prepare icing: In medium saucepan, blend eggs with sugar, stirring well to combine. Combine remaining ingredients with eggs. Cook over medium heat until mixture is thickened. Remove from heat.

When cake is out of oven, stir in coconut and nuts, if using. Spread icing over hot cake. Makes one 13-by-9-inch cake.

Note: This cake is very good served warm but will be tricky to remove from pan. Use a slender, offset spatula to lift cake pieces from pan.

SHERRY CREAM CAKE

Not really a cake, but a trifle, this dessert is still known as a Sherry Cream Cake. It's popular in Savannah, Ga., where ladies' societies set it out at tea time and for coffee with special guests.

1 small envelope unflavored
   gelatin
1/2 cup water
5 extra-large egg yolks
3/4 cup sugar, divided use
3/4 cup dry sherry
1/4 cup water
2 cups heavy cream, chilled
1 tablespoon vanilla extract

TO ASSEMBLE
1 angel food cake, cut into
   1 1/2-inch cubes
1 cup fresh strawberries,
   sliced
1 cup fresh raspberries
1/2 cup blueberries
2 tablespoons sugar
Whipped cream
Mint leaves, if desired

In a small bowl, sprinkle the gelatin into 1/2 cup of cold water to dissolve.

In a medium bowl, beat the egg yolks and 1/2 cup sugar until the mixture thickens and turns pale yellow, about two minutes. Stir in the sherry and 1/4 cup water.

Put the yolk mixture into a heavy-bottomed saucepan and cook over medium-low heat, stirring constantly, until the custard thickens. Mixture should coat back of spoon. Caution: Do not allow mixture to boil.

Pour the custard into a large bowl and stir in the gelatin; set aside to cool slightly.

In a large bowl, whip 2 cups of cream until it begins to thicken. Gradually beat in 1/4 cup of the sugar and vanilla. Beat until stiff peaks hold. Cover and chill whipped cream.

Set the bowl containing the custard and gelatin into a large bowl of ice water. Stir until the custard is cold and begins to thicken, three to four minutes. Remove from the ice and fold in the whipped cream.

In a greased 10-inch tube pan, alternately layer the cake and custard, starting with cake and ending with custard, making sure cake is well covered with custard. Cover and refrigerate until set, one to two hours.

Combine berries in a large bowl and sprinkle with sugar, about 2 tablespoons. Refrigerate to draw out juices.

When ready to serve, unmold cake onto serving platter. (Use a knife dipped in hot water to run around edge of cake to loosen.) Slice cake and serve with berries and whipped cream. Garnish with mint leaves, if desired.

Makes one 10-inch tube pan cake.

Note: This is a good cake for making in advance; it's best eaten after two days of refrigeration.

SOUR MILK CHOCOLATE CAKE

In the following cake, you can easily substitute buttermilk for the sour milk. Even better is "old" buttermilk, which has more tang than fresh buttermilk. Let it sit in the refrigerator for three weeks or so to develop its tang. Shake well before using.

CAKE
1/4 cup butter
1/2 cup brown sugar
1 1/2 cups sifted cake flour
1 teaspoon baking powder
1 teaspoon baking soda
2/3 cup sour milk
1 extra-large egg, beaten
1 teaspoon vanilla
2 squares unsweetened
  chocolate or 1/4 cup
  unsweetened cocoa powder

FROSTING
2/3 cup milk
2 cups granulated sugar
2 unsweetened chocolate
  squares
2 tablespoons corn syrup
2 tablespoons butter

Grease and flour two 8-inch cake pans; set aside. Preheat oven to 350 degrees F.

Cream butter and brown sugar in medium bowl of electric mixer on medium speed.

In smaller bowl, mix together with wire whisk the flour, baking powder and baking soda.

In measuring cup, mix milk, egg and vanilla.

Add flour mixture and milk mixture to creamed mixture, beginning and ending with the flour. Mix well to combine. Mix in chocolate.

Pour into prepared pans and bake at 350 degrees F until tops spring back when touched gently, about 25 minutes.

To make frosting: In medium, heavy-bottomed saucepan, cook sugar, corn syrup, chocolate and milk, stirring constantly, over medium heat until it forms a soft ball. Depending on weather, this may take up to 40 minutes. (A drop of the mixture in ice-cold water will hold together and sink to a soft ball in the bottom of the glass.)

Remove from heat; add vanilla and butter and beat to proper consistency. Frost between layers and top and sides.

Makes one 8-inch layer cake.

1-2-3-4 CAKE

This is the other "basic" cake found in most recipe boxes around the South. It's simple and typically put together with whatever frosting or fruit was available. Because it makes a nice three-layer cake, I use it for the Fresh Orange Cake, traditional at the holiday. As with the pound cake, its name refers to the ingredient measurements.

1 cup butter	2 teaspoons baking powder
2 cups sugar, divided use	1 cup milk
4 eggs, separated	1 teaspoon vanilla extract
3 cups cake flour	

Preheat oven to 350 degrees F. Grease and flour three 9-inch cake pans.

In a large bowl, cream butter with 1 cup of sugar until light. Add egg yolks, one at a time beating well after each is added.

Sift together flour and baking powder onto a sheet of waxed paper.

Add the flour alternately with the milk to the butter mix, beating well. Add vanilla and beat until incorporated.

In a medium bowl, beat egg whites until soft peaks form. Add remaining cup of sugar and beat until stiff, but not dry. Use a rubber spatula to fold the whites into the batter.

Spoon batter into prepared pans and bake at 350 degrees F for 20 to 25 minutes, or until toothpick comes out clean.

Makes three 9-inch layers. These layers freeze well.

PIES

CRUST FOR 10-INCH PIE

A good crust makes a good pie. Too many cooks buy ready-made, and while their quality has improved, they're still nothing like the homemade, fresh flaky pastry everyone expects. Here's the basic crust. Handling it as little as possible and using just enough flour to get it to come together is crucial. Chilling it before rolling out also helps keep it flaky.

1 cup flour
5 tablespoons chilled lard or vegetable shortening

1 teaspoon salt
2 or 3 tablespoons, as needed, ice water

Put all ingredients except water in food processor fitted with metal blade. Process by long pulses until mixture has texture of coarse cornmeal. With motor running, add water a tablespoon at a time until dough gathers in a loose ball around the blade. If you need more water, add only a sprinkle at a time – do not overprocess. Remove from bowl.

Place ball on plastic wrap and flatten to a disk shape. Wrap and chill for 30 minutes before using.

To roll out, place disk on a lightly floured surface. Rub rolling pin with flour and roll from center of disk outward, giving dough a quarter turn at each roll. Roll to about 1/8-inch thick and about 2 1/2 inches larger than pie plate. Fold dough over itself and lift, using rolling pin, into pie plate. Unfold gently, pressing dough into bottom of plate to avoid air bubbles.

Finish pie crust edge by crimping or "roping" with fingers, or use a fork to score it attractively. Trim unwanted dough with a sharp knife.

Chill pie crust until using.

To bake a crust "blind" for filling with unbaked filling fruit or custards:

Place crust in pie pan as indicated above. Preheat oven to 425 degrees F. Use a fork to prick sides and bottom of pie crust well, piercing through crust to the pan.

Place waxed paper sheet on top of pie crust and fill with pie weights or dried beans (to prevent crust from rising). Bake at 425 degrees F until medium-brown, 15-18 minutes. Watch carefully to prevent burning. Remove and chill before filling.

Makes 1 crust.

BANANA CREAM PIE

Other than the coconut cream pie, the banana cream is the one most likely to appear at diners, truck stops, etc. The banana liqueur gives this a little oomph. You can leave it out or substitute vanilla.

1/2 cup sugar
1/4 cup cornstarch
Dash salt
1 cup heavy (whipping) cream
1 cup milk
3 egg yolks, lightly beaten
3 tablespoons unsalted butter, at room temperature
2 ripe (but still firm) bananas

3 tablespoons banana liqueur

TOPPING
1 1/2 cups heavy whipping cream
2 tablespoons powdered sugar
1 teaspoon vanilla extract
1 prebaked 9-inch pie crust

In heavy saucepan, whisk together cornstarch, sugar and salt. Add cream slowly, whisking to combine sugar. Add milk and whisk; add yolks individually, whisking to combine.

Cook over medium heat, stirring constantly, until mixture comes to a gentle boil. Reduce heat and cook, still stirring constantly, for about three minutes or until mixture is well thickened. Pour through a strainer into a large mixing bowl.

Add butter and stir to melt.

Cover with layer of plastic wrap that seals to surface of mixture. Cool on the counter to room temperature.

Slice bananas and put in bottom of pie crust. Whisk custard mixture and stir in banana liqueur. Spoon mixture over bananas; smooth top of pie. Chill pie for 30 minutes.

Make topping: In medium, chilled bowl, beat cream until soft peaks form. Add sugar gradually, beating continuously until stiff peaks form. Add vanilla and beat. Mound on top of well-chilled pie.

Refrigerate until completely chilled through.

Makes one 9-inch pie. Pie will freeze, but is best eaten fresh. Refrigerate leftovers.

BROWN SUGAR PIE

Brown sugar pies are peculiar. They're almost a pecan pie without the pecans. A molasses pie is similar. The addition of nutmeg gives clues that this was possibly a leftover from Colonial days.

2 eggs
1/2 teaspoon salt
2 cups brown sugar, loosely spooned into cup   not packed
5 tablespoons unsalted butter, melted
1 cup milk

1 tablespoon cornstarch
1 teaspoon nutmeg
Dash nutmeg for top of pie
1 9-inch prebaked crust (bake only to tan-white stage; do not brown)

Preheat oven to 350 degrees F.

In medium mixing bowl, beat together eggs and salt. Add brown sugar and mix well. Add butter and combine.

In measuring cup, combine milk and cornstarch; stir until smooth. Beat with slow mixer into sugar mixture. Add nutmeg and mix. Pour all ingredients into partially baked pie crust; dust top of pie with nutmeg.

Bake at 350 degrees F for 30 minutes or until filling is set.

Remove and cool to room temperature; chill well before slicing.

Makes one 9-inch pie.

BUTTERMILK PIE

Buttermilk used to be a staple of Southern kitchens; it was used in making the daily pans of biscuits and often, cornbread. It's only natural that it would also show up as a pie ingredient. Don't let the name fool you, however; it's lemon-flavored and, with the buttermilk, has that perfect tang.

1 cup sugar	1/2 cup butter (1 stick)
3 eggs	1/2 cup buttermilk
1/2 tablespoon flour	1 9-inch unbaked pie crust
2 tablespoons lemon extract	

Preheat oven to 375 degrees F.

In large mixing bowl, combine ingredients in order given, beating to combine. Do not overbeat. Pour into unbaked pie crust and bake for 15 minutes at 375 degrees F. Turn oven down to 350 degrees F and bake for 30 minutes more or until filling is set in center.

Makes one 9-inch pie. Pie freezes well; refrigerate leftovers.

CHESS PIE

Along with pecan, chess pies are probably the most well-known Southern pies. Chess (the origin of the word is controversial; some think it means cheese, others say it refers to the keeping quality of the pies) pies are found throughout Appalachia.

3 eggs
1 1/2 cups sugar
1/2 cup unsalted butter or margarine, at room temperature
1 tablespoon cornmeal

1 tablespoon all purpose flour
1 teaspoon vinegar
4 tablespoons milk
1 teaspoon vanilla
1 unbaked 9-inch pie crust

Preheat oven to 375 degrees F.

In a medium mixing bowl, beat eggs just until combined. Add sugar and beat; add butter and beat to combine. By hand, stir in meal and flour. Combine vinegar, milk and vanilla in a small measuring cup and add to mixture; beat until smooth.

Pour into an unbaked 9-inch pie crust. Bake at 375 degrees F for 20 minutes; lower oven to 350 degrees and bake for approximately 40 minutes or until filling is set in center. If needed, cover crust with foil to prevent overbrowning.

Makes one 9-inch pie.

51

CHOCOLATE PECAN PIE

2/3 cup evaporated milk
2 tablespoons butter or
  margarine
1 (16-ounce) package semi-
sweet chocolate morsels
2 eggs, beaten
1 cup sugar

2 tablespoon all-purpose flour
1/4 teaspoon salt
1 teaspoon vanilla
1 cup chopped pecans
1 unbaked 9-inch deep dish
  pie crust

Preheat oven to 375 degrees F.

In a heavy saucepan over low heat, combine milk, butter and chocolate pieces. Stir until chocolate is melted; remove from heat.

In a mixing bowl, beat eggs and sugar on low. Add flour, salt, and vanilla and combine. Add chocolate mixture, mixing well. Stir in pecans.

Pour mixture into unbaked pie crust. Bake at 375 degrees F for 40 minutes. Filling may puff slightly, then fall; this is normal. Pie will freeze well; refrigerate leftovers.

CHOCOLATE SILK PIE

The silky smooth texture of this pie gives it its name. As with many other pies baked in the South, the recipe specifically mentions Pet milk. The brand name has become synonymous with evaporated milk; many handwritten recipes call merely for Pet milk, leaving some newer cooks confused.

1 1/2 cups sugar
3 tablespoons unsweetened
   cocoa powder
3 eggs, beaten
2/3 cup Pet milk (evaporated
   milk)

1/2 cup butter or margarine,
   melted
1 teaspoon vanilla extract
Sweetened whipped cream,
   for serving
1 unbaked 9-inch pie crust

In medium bowl, whisk together sugar and cocoa powder. Whisk in eggs, milk and   butter to combine. Add vanilla and mix well.

Pour into pie crust. Bake at 350 degrees F for 30 to 35 minutes or until center rises and crust edges are browned.

Cool on rack to room temperature; chill until firm in refrigerator.

Serve with sweetened whipped cream

Makes one 9-inch pie. This pie freezes well. Refrigerate leftovers.

COCONUT CREAM PIE

This is a pie you expect to find in any diner or along the road in Southern coffee shops and local cafeteria lines. A generation or two ago, cooks might have resorted to a pudding filling and you still could substitute one. But here's the real deal. It has nothing fake in it, just pure flavor. Note: Using the sweetened, bagged coconut in place of fresh will make it extra sweet, but the sugar is essential to the custard texture, so don't attempt to reduce it.

3/4 cup cornstarch
1 1/2 cups sugar
1/2 teaspoon salt
4 cups milk, scalded (heat until small bubbles form around edges)
2 eggs, slightly beaten
1 teaspoon vanilla

2 tablespoons butter
1 teaspoon coconut extract
1 cup coarsely shredded fresh coconut
1 prebaked 10-inch pie shell, chilled
4 cups whipped cream, for topping

In medium, heavy bottomed saucepan, whisk together cornstarch, sugar and salt. Scald milk in small saucepan, and gradually stir scalded milk into the sugar mixture. Whisk to combine and dissolve sugar. Bring mixture to a boil over medium heat, stirring constantly. Boil until thick and glossy, about three minutes.

Put eggs in small bowl. Add a few spoonfuls of the hot sugar mixture to the eggs, stirring well to bring them to a higher temperature. Add the eggs back to the hot mixture slowly, stirring constantly. With an electric mixer, beat at medium speed for two minutes, still cooking over medium heat. Watch to prevent mixture from curdling. Mixture should be thickened.

Remove saucepan from heat and add vanilla and butter, stirring in until smooth and creamy.

Pour mixture into a bowl through a strainer to remove any lumps. Place a layer of plastic wrap directly on surface of custard, and cool to room temperature.

Once custard is cool, add coconut extract and of the coconut; mix well to combine.

Pour filling into prebaked crust. Chill completely.

When ready to serve, spoon whipped cream over top of pie and swirl decoratively. Sprinkle remaining coconut flakes over center of pie.

Makes 1 10-inch pie. Refrigerate leftovers.

DINAH SHORE'S "LETHAL" PECAN PIE

Pecan groves dot the Southern landscape from Texas to north Florida, and into the South Carolina latitude. A good pecan pie is a requisite of every cook's staple recipe book. This one is attributed to a native of Tennessee, the famous singer known for her Southern hospitality, Dinah Shore.

1 1/4 cups dark corn syrup
1 cup firmly packed light brown sugar
4 tablespoons unsalted butter
4 large eggs
1 teaspoon pure vanilla extract

2 1/2 cups broken or coarsely chopped pecans
1/4 teaspoon salt
1 9-inch unbaked deep pie shell

Preheat oven to 350 degrees F.

In a 1-quart saucepan over medium heat, combine corn syrup and sugar. Cook, stirring, until sugar has dissolved. Allow mixture to boil for two to three minutes; remove from heat and stir in butter.

In large mixing bowl of stand mixer, beat eggs well. Continue to beat while slowly adding boiled syrup mixture. Stir in vanilla, pecans and salt.

To prevent spilling, pour only half of mixture into unbaked pie shell; place on baking sheet in center rack of oven. Pour in remaining mixture and bake 45-50 minutes, or until filling has set. Note: You may need to wrap crust edges in foil to prevent burning.

Remove, cool to room temperature and chill well before slicing.

Makes one 9-inch pie.

Pie will freeze well; keep leftovers refrigerated.

FRIED PIES

I've included fried pies in this chapter, because they are a type of fruit pie. Unique to the South, they are found at certain barbecue joints, church gatherings and out-of-the-way eateries. The best are home-made, however, and filled with dried apples, peach or leftover sweet potatoes (mashed). I firmly believe they should be eaten as warm as possible, but take care; the filling is so hot, it can cause serious burns.

FILLING
2 packages of dried apples
　or peaches
Water to cover
2/3 cup sugar, or to taste
1/2 teaspoon cinnamon
1/2 tablespoon lemon juice

DOUGH
1 can refrigerated flaky-style
　biscuit dough
Flour
Oil for frying
Powdered sugar for dusting,
　as desired

Make filling: Put apples in medium heavy-bottomed sauce-pan. Add water to cover fruit. Bring to a boil; reduce heat to simmer and cook until apples are plump and tender. Pour off all but one tablespoon water. Add sugar to taste, and stir well. Add cinnamon; cool.

Make the pies: On a floured board, roll out each biscuit to a round of about 5 inches. Place a tablespoon or so of cooked apples on half of the dough; fold other half of dough over to form a half-moon. Seal edges very well with fingers or fork. Repeat with remaining biscuits and fruit filling. Set pies on baking sheet and chill for 30 minutes.

Heat oil in heavy pan to 375 degrees F. Fry pies, only two at a time, until well browned and puffy, turning once with slotted spoon to fry both sides. Drain on absorbent paper. Dust with confectioner's sugar.

Serve warm. Caution: Filling is extremely hot coming from fryer and will burn skin and mouth if dripped.

Makes 12 pies.

GEORGIA PEACH PIE

A Georgia peach pie, served warm with (preferably) homemade ice cream, is the ultimate summer treat. Use good fresh peaches, still mostly firm, with strong scent for best results.

8 ripe, firm peaches, peeled, sliced
1/2 cup sugar
1/4 cup flour
2 tablespoons freshly squeezed lemon juice

1/2 teaspoon cinnamon, optional
Milk, for brushing pie top
1 unbaked 9-inch deep-dish pie crust for 2-crust pie

Preheat oven to 375 degrees F.

In large bowl, toss together peach slices, sugar, ¨ cup flour, lemon juice, and cinnamon, if desired.

Put filling into bottom crust. Cut remaining crust into 1 1/2-inch strips. Form lattice top by weaving strips over top of pie. Seal ends of strips to bottom crust edges. Brush pie top with milk.

Bake 50 minutes or until filling is bubbling and crust is nicely browned.

Makes one 9-inch pie.

Pie freezes well.

GRAPEFRUIT PIE

A grapefruit pie is a favorite winter dessert in certain areas of Texas. Most of us don't think of citrus fruits when we consider Texas; however, they grow a great deal of it in their southernmost areas. A pink grapefruit makes this a pretty pie, but it can be made with any grapefruit variety.

1 cup water
1 cup sugar
3 tablespoons cornstarch
Dash salt
3/4 cup grapefruit juice
2 egg yolks
1 9-inch pie crust, prebaked
and chilled

MERINGUE
2 egg whites
1/4 cup sugar
1 1/2 teaspoon grated lemon
rind (zest)

In a medium saucepan over medium-high heat, mix sugar, water and a half cup of the grapefruit juice. Bring to a boil.

In a measuring cup, combine remaining 1/4 cup grapefruit juice with cornstarch and salt; add to boiling syrup. Boil until mixture thickens slightly. Remove from heat.

Beat egg yolks in a small bowl; add 2 tablespoons of the hot syrup and stir to bring the yolks to temperature. Slowly add the heated yolks into the syrup, stirring constantly to prevent the yolks from cooking.

Pour mixture into prebaked pie crust.

Make meringue: In medium mixing bowl, beat egg whites until soft peaks hold. Add sugar and beat to incorporate. Whip in lemon zest. Spread over pie to edges of crust. Bake at 400 degrees F until lightly browned, about 10 minutes. Watch carefully to prevent burning.

Makes one 9-inch pie.

GREEN TOMATO PIE

By now, most people know about fried green tomatoes and their strong association with the South. Green tomatoes are also made into pies here, but few people will know what is really in this pie if you don't tell them. The flavor is that of a green apple, but the texture is more like that of a peach. It's put together like an apple pie; you can use an apple pie spice mixture if you prefer.

1 pound green tomatoes, sliced thinly	Dash salt
1/3 cup sugar	1 tablespoon white vinegar
1/2 teaspoon cinnamon	1 1/2 teaspoons flour
1/2 teaspoon allspice	1 unbaked 9-inch pie crust for
1/4 teaspoon ground cloves	a two-crust pie

Preheat oven to 425 F.

Put sliced tomatoes in bottom of pie crust. Mix sugar with spices and salt; sprinkle mixture over tomatoes. Sprinkle with vinegar and flour. Top with second crust, crimping together edges of crust. Make several vents in pie, including center.

Bake at 425 degrees F until crust is golden. Cool pie at room temperature; chill well for best slicing, or serve warm.

Makes one 9-inch pie. This pie freezes well. Refrigerate leftovers.

KENTUCKY HORSE RACE PIE

The Kentucky Derby folks have trademarked the name of the pie that's traditionally served at all Derby events. Smart folks. Of course, we've seen dozens of variations; this is fairly close to the original, we're pretty sure. And to prevent any legal action, we'll call this the Kentucky Horse Race Pie. By any name, it's a run-for-the-roses winner.

4 eggs
3/4 cup white sugar
1/4 cup brown sugar
1 teaspoon vanilla
2 to 4 tablespoons bourbon
3/4 cup light corn syrup
1/2 cup butter, melted

1 tablespoon flour
1 generous cup chopped pecans
1 generous cup chocolate chip pieces
1 unbaked 9-inch deep-dish pie shell

Preheat oven to 350 degrees F.

In large mixing bowl, beat eggs till light. Add sugars and vanilla; beat well. Add bourbon, corn syrup, melted butter and flour and beat at medium speed until combined.

Toss together pecans and chocolate pieces in small bowl; pour into unbaked pie crust. Pour sugar and egg mixture over nuts and chocolate. (Nuts may float; this is normal.)

Bake at 350 degrees F for 35 to 40 minutes or until filling is set.

Makes one 9-inch pie. This pie freezes well after baking. Refrigerate any leftovers.

KEY LIME PIE, TRADITIONAL

Being from South Florida, I grew up assuming everyone had Key limes and made Key lime pie. It's only since the juice of the golf-ball-shaped yellow limes has been marketed nationally that the pie has traveled to all corners. And a word of caution: Never, ever tint the pie green – real Key lime juice yields a pale yellow color.

1 can (14 ounces) sweetened
   condensed milk
3 egg yolks, beaten
1/2 cup plus 2 tablespoons
   Key lime juice
1 teaspoon grated rind of limes,
   for garnish

1 9-inch pie crust, prebaked
   (see notes)
Whipped cream for serving,
   as desired

In a medium mixing bowl, combine milk, eggs and Key lime juice. Beat well until   smooth. Pour into cooled, prebaked crust.

Refrigerate until filling is set. Serve with whipped cream and lime zest as desired.

Makes one 9-inch pie. These pies freeze very well. Refrigerate any leftovers.

Notes: You can use a graham-cracker crust if desired; traditionally, a pastry pie crust was used and some prefer it. Note, however, that the crust must be completely cooled before adding filling.

If you are worried about using raw egg yolks in this recipe, use pasteurized eggs, found in most supermarkets or natural-food stores. These have been heated to kill any harmful bacteria. You also can bake the pie at 350 degrees F for 15 minutes to bring the eggs to a safe temperature.

KEY LIME PIE WITH CREAM CHEESE

This is another version of the Key lime; it also leads into a lemon cream cheese pie. It's guaranteed to come out firm.

1 can sweetened condensed milk (14 ounces)
2 egg yolks, slightly beaten
  – no egg whites, they cause runny pies
1/2 cup fresh lime juice
1 tablespoon grated lime rind
4 ounces (1/2 of a large package) cream cheese, at room temperature
1 9-inch prebaked pie crust (or use graham cracker crust)

In the bowl of an electric mixer, combine condensed milk, lime juice, lime rind and eggs; beat well. Beat in cream cheese until lemon colored. Pour mixture into prepared crust and refrigerate until firm.

Makes one 9-inch pie. This pie freezes well; refrigerate any leftovers.

For lemon cream cheese pie: Substitute 1/2 cup lemon juice and grated rind of lemon for the Key limes. Use egg whites to make a meringue for this pie if desired: Beat 2 egg whites until foamy; add two tablespoons sugar, beating until soft peaks are formed. Spread to edges of pie; bake at 400 degrees F until lightly browned (watch carefully to prevent burning). Cool briefly and refrigerate.

LEMON CHESS PIE

This version of chess pie, known in some areas as "Confederate Pie," includes lemon a favorite flavoring when others aren't available. Take care to beat the filling only until combined, or the pie will separate into two layers when baked not the desired result.

1/2 cup butter
1 1/2 cups sugar
1 teaspoon flour
1/8 teaspoon salt
2 tablespoons milk

1 lemon, juice and grated rind (zest)
3 whole eggs, slightly beaten
1 unbaked 9-inch pie crust

In a large mixing bowl, cream together softened butter and sugar. Add flour, mixing well. Add remaining ingredients and beat until smooth, but do not overbeat or mixture will separate as it bakes.

Bake at 325 degrees F for 45 to 55 minutes or until filling is set. If need, cover crust edges with foil to prevent overbrowning. This pie freezes well.

Makes one 9-inch pie.

LEMON MERINGUE PIE

*I know of no diner, truck stop or café that doesn't have a lemon
meringue pie on its menu. Sadly, many people have never tasted a
homemade one; it's too easy to buy one or buy a pudding to make the
filling. Make the real thing just once: You'll be a convert for life.*

1 1/2 cups sugar
1/3 cup plus 1 tablespoon
  cornstarch
1 1/2 cups water
3 egg yolks, beaten
3 tablespoons butter
1/2 cup fresh lemon juice

MERINGUE
3 egg whites, room temperature
1/4 teaspoon cream of tartar
6 tablespoons sugar
1/2 teaspoon vanilla extract
1 prebaked 9-inch pie crust

Combine sugar and cornstarch in a heavy-bottomed medium
saucepan. Stir in water slowly to dissolve sugar.

Cook over medium heat, stirring constantly until mixture
thickens; allow to boil for   one minute, stirring constantly. Remove from heat while ladling a few spoons of the hot mixture
into the beaten egg yolks, stirring them to prevent curdling.

Pour hot egg mixture back into saucepan gradually, stirring
quickly to prevent the eggs from cooking. Heat mixture to a
slow boil, stirring constantly; cook one minute. Remove from
heat. Cool for five minutes. Stir in butter and lemon juice, mixing well. Pour into prepared crust.

Remove from heat; stir in butter and lemon juice, mixing
well. Pour into baked pie crust. Allow to cool on counter while
you make meringue:

In medium bowl of mixer, beat egg whites and cream of tartar
until soft peaks form. Beat in sugar gradually at high speed,
beating until peaks are stiff and glossy. Add vanilla; beat again.

Spoon meringue over warm pie filling; spread meringue to touch edges of crust to prevent shrinking.

Bake at 400 degrees F, for about seven minutes or until meringue is a golden brown (take care not to overbake or meringue will burn). Cool on counter for about 30 minutes; refrigerate until well chilled.

Makes one 9-inch pie. This pie can be frozen but may become soggy on thawing. It's best eaten when freshly made.

PEANUT BUTTER PIE

A peanut butter pie is a thing of beauty to many pie lovers. Getting the "chiffon" texture just right is part of the trick. In this pie, cream cheese and whipped cream are combined to give it the lift. It's not as overly sweet as those made with a frozen dairy topping.

4 tablespoons cream cheese
1 cup powdered sugar
1/3 cup half-and-half
1 teaspoon vanilla
1 cup smooth peanut butter
1 1/2 cups heavy whipping cream

Chopped peanuts, for garnish if desired
1 9-inch graham cracker crust (or chocolate cookie crumb crust)

In a mixing bowl of electric mixer, beat together cream cheese and powdered sugar. Beat in half-and-half and vanilla; cream in peanut butter.

In a separate chilled bowl, whip the heavy cream until very thick, stiff peaks form and cream sticks to beaters when lifted. Spoon about 1/3 of the whipped cream into the peanut butter mixture, mixing in on low speed. Remove from mixer and using rubber spatula, fold in remaining whipped cream.

66

Spoon mixture into crust. Refrigerate or freeze. If freezing, thaw to room temperature before slicing. Decorate slices with chopped peanuts, if desired.

Makes one 9-inch pie. Refrigerate leftovers.

PECAN PIE WITH CREAM CHEESE

The addition of a fluffy cream cheese layer makes this pecan pie different.

8-ounce package cream cheese,
    softened (not whipped cream cheese)
4 eggs
1/3 plus 1/4 cup sugar
1 teaspoon vanilla

1 9-inch unbaked deep-dish pie shell
1 1/4 cups coarsely chopped pecans
1 cup light corn syrup
1 teaspoon vanilla
1/4 teaspoon salt

Preheat oven to 350 degrees F.

In medium mixing bowl, cream together cream cheese, one egg, 1/3 cup sugar, and 1 teaspoon vanilla. Spread mixture on bottom of unbaked pie shell.

Sprinkle chopped pecans over cream cheese mixture. In medium mixing bowl, beat remaining three eggs until combined. Add corn syrup, 1/4 cup sugar, 1 teaspoon vanilla and salt and mix well. Pour mixture over pecans.

Bake in preheated oven for 40 minutes or until nuts are slightly browned.

Note: Top of pie may rise in oven and fall once removed; this is normal.

Cool to room temperature and chill well before slicing; makes 1 9-inch pie. Note: this serves eight easily. It's a very rich pie.

This pie freezes well. Keep leftovers refrigerated.

PUMPKIN-PECAN PIE

As mentioned, pecan pies are traditional on the Thanksgiving table, and so is pumpkin. Bright cooks have combined the two for this pie.

3 eggs, beaten
1 cup pumpkin puree
  (canned pumpkin)
1 cup sugar
1/2 cup dark corn syrup
1 teaspoon vanilla
1/2 teaspoon pumpkin pie
  spice

1/4 teaspoon salt
1 cup pecans, coarsely
chopped
1 unbaked 9-inch deep-dish
  pie crust

Preheat oven to 350 F.

In large mixing bowl, beat eggs slightly. Add pumpkin, beating well. Add sugar, corn syrup and vanilla; mix well to blend. Toss pecans with salt and spices and mix in on low speed until combined.

Pour mixture into unbaked pie shell and place in bottom third of oven. Bake for about 40 minutes or until center of pie no longer appears "wet."

Remove and cool on rack; chill well before serving.

Makes one 9-inch pie.

This pie can be frozen but is best when eaten fresh. Refrigerate any leftovers.

STRAWBERRY PIE

Florida's Pant City is one of the winter strawberry capitals in the United States. So down here, we make this pie in February and March. Most others will make it toward the end of spring. Avoid the urge to buy that goop they sell in supermarkets to coat a strawberry pie. It's easy enough to make your own thickener without all those additives.

3 tablespoons cornstarch
3/4 cup sugar
Dash salt
1 cup water
1 tablespoon butter
1 tablespoon lemon juice

1 teaspoon liqueur, as desired (see note)
1 9-inch prebaked pie crust (or use graham cracker as desired)

In medium saucepan, combine cornstarch, sugar and salt. Add water and bring mixture to a slow boil over medium-high heat. Cook, stirring, until mixture is thickened and clear. Add butter, lemon juice and liqueur if using, and stir to combine. Cool.

Prepare berries: wash, clean, slice in half and place in colander. Catch any juice to color whipped cream, if desired.

Put berries into cooled pie shell and pour thickened sugar mixture over top. Chill well to set. Serve with whipped cream or as desired.

Makes one 9-inch pie.

Note: To flavor the thickened sauce poured over the berries, use Framboise, Frangelica, Cointreau or any other fruit-based liqueur. One tablespoon is adequate; stir in after removing from heat. Alternately, toss the berries with the liqueur before adding to pie crust.

SWEET POTATO PIE

Sweet potato pie is another Thanksgiving standard, with some of my relatives preferring its flavor to pumpkin. It's also a must at Sunday dinners-on-the grounds and most family reunions. Most good barbecue eateries serve it as their only dessert. Evaporated milk – not sweetened condensed milk – makes this pie what it is. Don't even think of substituting.

3 large sweet potatoes
1/2 cup (1 stick) unsalted butter
3 eggs, beaten
2 cups sugar
1/2 teaspoon cinnamon
(optional)

2/3 cup (1 small can)
  evaporated milk
1 1/2 tablespoons cornstarch
1 1/2 teaspoons vanilla extract
3 unbaked 9-inch pie crusts

In medium pot, boil the scrubbed sweet potatoes in water to cover. When potatoes are tender, drain and cool. Peel potatoes.

In large mixing bowl, beat potatoes with butter until smooth. Add eggs and milk and beat well. In a small bowl, combine sugar, cinnamon if using, and cornstarch; add to potatoes, beating to combine. Add vanilla and beat well.

Divide mixture between three 9-inch unbaked pie crusts.

(Note: Pies will freeze well at this point and can be baked directly from freezer as desired.)

Bake at 350 degrees F for about 45 minutes or until filling sets.

Makes three 9-inch pies. These pies freeze well; keep leftovers refrigerated.

Puddings, Cobblers & Other Delicacies

BANANA PUDDING

Bananas aren't found growing throughout the South, but you won't get far in the region without seeing banana pudding on some menu, and you probably won't attend a family reunion without seeing one.

This is another case when you can use boxed pudding mixes and frozen whipped topping, but it really cheats on the flavor. Just don't skimp on the bananas, either way.

CUSTARD
1 1/2 cups sugar
2 heaping tablespoons flour
1/4 teaspoon salt
4 eggs, separated
3 cups whole milk (see note)
3 tablespoons butter
1 teaspoon vanilla

LAYERS
4 ripe bananas, sliced
1 box vanilla wafers

MERINGUE
4 egg whites, room temperature
1/3 cup sugar
1/4 teaspoon cream of tartar
1 teaspoon vanilla

Note: While low-fat milk is OK, skim milk will produce a watery pudding. If you wish, use evaporated skim milk to add the richness the custard requires.

In heavy-bottomed saucepan, combine sugar, flour, and salt. In a small bowl, beat egg yolks (reserve whites for meringue) with milk; combine with dry ingredients, stirring well. Place pot over medium heat and cook, stirring constantly. When sugar is dissolved, add butter and continue to cook, stirring, until thickened (mixture will easily coat back of spoon).

Remove from heat and stir in vanilla. Set aside to cool slightly.

Lightly grease the inside of a 2-quart ovenproof dish or

oblong baking pan. Place a layer of vanilla wafers on bottom of pan, add a layer of bananas, and a layer of custard. Repeat until all wafers, banana slices and custard are used, with custard being the top layer.

Make meringue: In spotlessly clean bowl, beat egg whites until soft peaks form. Gradually add sugar, a little at a time, beating well. Add sugar and mix again. Mixture will turn glossy and foam appearance will be soft. Whisk in cream of tartar to stabilize.

Spoon meringue onto top of cooled custard, sealing well to edges.

Bake at 400 degrees F for 8 minutes or until meringue is lightly browned.

Chill very well before serving, or serve warm.

Makes 8 servings.

BREAD PUDDING WITH BOURBON SAUCE

Bread pudding is a classic New Orleans favorite. Leftover crusty French bread or similar bread makes the best pudding texture, but Danish or croissants also work very well. A bourbon sauce is a must, and if the pudding is served warm, ice cream is a great idea as well.

1 loaf stale French bread, torn into bite-size chunks	2 tablespoons butter, softened
	1 tablespoon vanilla
1 quart milk	1/2 cup raisins
4 eggs	Bourbon Sauce
2 cups sugar	(recipe follows)

Note: You will need a 13-by-9-inch baking pan, and a larger shallow roasting pan to contain water for baking.

Preheat oven to 350 degrees. Grease a 13-by-9-inch baking

73

dish; set aside.

Put torn bread cubes into a large bowl and cover with milk. Stir. Let stand until most of milk is absorbed.

In a medium bowl, beat together eggs and sugar until well combined. Add butter, mixing well. Add vanilla and raisins if using. Stir well.

Pour over bread mixture, stirring well to combine. Pour mixture into prepared baking dish and place dish in roasting pan; set on bottom rack of oven. Pour water into roasting pan.

Bake at 350 degrees F for 1-1/4 hours, or until a knife inserted in pudding comes out clean.

Remove pudding pan carefully from roaster in oven; pan may drip hot water. Cool slightly on rack before serving.

Serve with Bourbon Sauce and whipped cream, as desired.

BOURBON SAUCE

6 tablespoons butter	**1 egg yolk, beaten**
1 small can evaporated milk	**1 teaspoon vanilla**
1 cup sugar	**1/3 cup good bourbon**

In top of double boiler over simmering water, combine butter and milk. Cook until butter melts. Stir a little milk into beaten yolk and stir heated yolk into milk mixture. Stir constantly until combined to prevent egg from cooking. Cook, stirring constantly, until mixture thickens to a sauce consistency.

Remove from heat and cool to lukewarm; slowly whisk in vanilla and bourbon until well combined. Drizzle over puddings.

STEAMED PERSIMMON PUDDING
WITH BRANDY SAUCE

*Persimmons grow throughout the mid South. It's a rite of passage in
childhood to be taunted into biting into a green persimmon — the
most sour and bitter of all fruits. Ripe ones are sweet, even honey like,
and make a fine pudding, however. It's a favorite Thanksgiving dessert
in some parts of the South.*

1 cup raisins
1/2 cup brandy
2 large persimmons
1 1/3 cups sugar
2 tablespoons butter, softened
1 cup plus 3 tablespoons
  all-purpose flour
1 teaspoon baking soda
1/2 teaspoon salt
1 teaspoon cinnamon
1/4 teaspoon cloves
1/4 teaspoon nutmeg

1/4 teaspoon allspice
1 cup chopped walnuts
1/2 cup half-and-half
2 egg whites
Brandy Sauce (recipe follows)
Whipped cream for serving,
  as desired

Note: You will need a 2-quart
pudding mold with lid, and a
large heavy pot to contain the
mold for steaming.

Liberally butter the inside and inner lid of a 2-quart pudding
mold. Shake granulated sugar into mold to coat; shake out
excess. Set aside.

Place a wire rack or heavy heat-proof footed trivet in bottom
of heavy pot to support pudding mold. Add enough water in pot
to reach two-thirds of the way to top of pudding mold when set
on rack. Cover pot, heat over medium-low to a simmer while

pudding is prepared.

Put raisins in a small bowl and pour brandy over them. Allow to sit until raisins are plump.

Peel and seed persimmons and place in bowl of food processor with metal blade, or in blender. Puree until smooth.

Put puree in a large mixer bowl. Add sugar and butter. Beat well to combine. In a separate smaller bowl, sift together flour, baking soda, salt and spices. Using a rubber spatula, fold the flour mixture into the puree mixture, mixing well. Stir in chopped nuts and raisin mixture. Gradually stir in half-and-half, mixing thoroughly. In a clean, small bowl, whip egg whites to soft peaks. Using rubber spatula, fold whites into pudding, using gentle strokes to lift pudding and keep air in eggs – do not beat.

Pour pudding mixture into greased mold. Run a knife through pudding to release trapped air bubbles. Place lid on mold. Use oven mitts or tongs to place pudding mold into pot of simmering water. (Steam should rise around all edges of mold.) Cover pot and gently steam pudding for 2 to 2-1/2 hours. Check pot every 20 minutes or so to make sure water level remains at about two-thirds the height of mold. If needed, add hot water.

To check for doneness, insert table knife in central portion of pudding; It will show some stickiness but not a runny batter.

Remove pudding from pot. Remove pudding mold lid, and cool pudding on a rack for 20 minutes. Turn pudding out directly onto serving platter. Serve warm, with brandy sauce and a dollop of whipped cream, if desired.

Makes 12 servings.

Note: This also can be made with plums.

BRANDY SAUCE

1/2 cup butter
1 cup sugar

1 egg
1/4 cup brandy

In top of a double boiler over low-simmering heat, combine butter and sugar. Stir until mixture is smooth and sugar is melted. Beat egg slightly in small cup. Add a tablespoon of the hot sugar mixture to egg, beating well to heat egg. Pour egg slowly into heated sugar mixture, stirring rapidly. Whisk in brandy and stir well.

Cook for two minutes over gently simmering heat, stirring constantly to prevent egg from cooking, or sauce will curdle.

Keep warm by placing over bowl of hot water. Serve with steamed puddings.

OLD-FASHIONED RICE PUDDING

Rice pudding is another diner dessert, not often found today, but well-loved as ever. It was originally intended as a way to use leftover rice, and that's still a good application. Raisins cause the biggest controversy, however, so ask guests whether they like their pudding with, or without. Solve the problem by adding raisins to half the mixture and chill in individual custard cups!

1 cup water	**3 eggs, well beaten**
1/2 cup uncooked rice, rinsed	**1/2 cup sugar**
4 tablespoons butter	**1/2 teaspoon vanilla**
4 cups milk	**1/2 cup raisins (optional)**

In medium saucepan, heat water to boiling; add rinsed rice. Cover and cook about five minutes without stirring. Remove lid and stir once. Add milk and butter; return to a boil. Stir. Reduce heat to low and cover. Cook for 45 minutes, stirring occasionally.

In medium mixing bowl, beat eggs with sugar; add vanilla. Add mixture to rice, stirring. Mixture will thicken as it cooks. Remove from heat when it reaches a thick but not stiff consistency. Stir in raisins, if desired.

Pour into buttered dish or mold; chill well. Serve with whipped cream or a sprinkle of cinnamon, if desired.

Makes 12 servings.

COBBLER, "MAGIC" BATTER-STYLE BERRY

There are some who whip up a kind of cake batter to go on top of the cobbler; this one is considered the "magic" batter because it's put on the bottom of the pan, but rises to the top as it bakes. It works with any berry, canned or fresh, or cherries

1/2 cup butter or stick-style margarine
1 cup self-rising flour
3/4 cup sugar
3/4 cup milk

2 cups fresh berries, rinsed well, picked over
1/2 teaspoon cinnamon
1/2 cup water
Whipped cream, if desired, for serving

Preheat oven to 350 degrees F. While oven is heating, put butter in a 1-1/2 quart baking pan and set in oven to melt. When butter is melted, remove and swirl to coat pan.

In mixing bowl, combine flour, half the sugar and milk. Mix well. Pour batter over butter in baking dish.

In large bowl, combine blueberries, the other half of sugar and water. Drop with spoon over batter in baking dish. Do not stir.

Bake at 350 degrees F for about 45 minutes, or until top is golden brown.

Serve warm, with whipped cream if desired.

COBBLER, BLACKBERRIES & DUMPLING

Cobblers are the least standardized of all Southern desserts. Often, a sweetened buttermilk or sweet milk biscuit dough is mixed up to top a bunch of fresh berries and sugar before baking.

4 cups blackberries, rinsed
   well (see note)
3/4 to 1 cup sugar, or to taste
   (depends on sweetness of
   berries)
1/4 teaspoon salt
1 teaspoon lemon juice

DUMPLINGS
1 1/2 cups flour
2 teaspoons baking powder
1 tablespoon sugar
1/4 teaspoon salt
Dash nutmeg or cinnamon
2/3 cup milk
Vanilla ice cream for serving

Preheat oven to 400 degrees F. In a heavy-bottomed oven-proof pot, combine berries, sugar, salt and lemon juice. Cook over medium heat, stirring until bubbly, about five minutes. Turn off heat.

In a mixing bowl, combine flour, baking powder, sugar, salt and spice, if using. Slowly add milk. Dough will be sticky and thick. Drop dough gently by tablespoons into blackberries to cover surface; do not stir.

Put pot in oven and bake for 35 to 45 minutes or until dumplings are lightly browned on top.

Serve from pot, scooping some berries and dumpling tops into each of six bowls.

Serve warm with vanilla ice cream. Makes six servings.

Note: Any time you're using fresh berries, try to include some underripe ones to add tartness to the cobbler. Other berries, such as blueberries or mulberries, work equally well in this dessert.

COBBLER, DISHPAN BLACKBERRY

In some old areas of the South, large enamel pans, most often referred to as "dishpans" are used in the kitchen for a multitude of chores. An enamel baking pan is therefore referred to as a dishpan, and a baked cobbler, covered with dough as a pot pie, is sometimes called a "dishpan pie" or a "dishpan cobbler." The dough can be made with buttermilk as a biscuit, but it's just as good with sweet milk.

1 1/2 cups self-rising flour
1/3 cup shortening
1 cup milk (sweet or buttermilk)
6 cups, approximately, fresh blackberries, rinsed well

4 cups sugar
3/4-1 cup of boiling water
4 tablespoons butter
1/4 cup flour
Vanilla ice cream for serving, if desired

Preheat oven to 350 degrees F.

In a medium bowl, combine flour and shortening, using pastry cutter or fingers to work shortening into flour. Add milk; work with hands to make a soft biscuit-style dough. Roll out dough on floured surface to about 1/4 inch thick.

Combine sugar and water; pour over berries. Mash berries slightly. Stir mixture to combine. Add butter. Pour mixture into greased 2-quart enamel "dishpan," baking dish or casserole. Sprinkle flour over all and stir very gently; some flour may be evident.

Put prepared dough over top of cobbler. Make a few small slashes in dough so juices can bubble through.

Bake at 350 degrees F until crust is golden brown, about 1 hour to 1 1/4 hours.

Serve hot with vanilla ice cream; makes eight servings.

COBBLER, PEACH

*Don't tell those fine folks of Georgia, but peaches grow all around
the South. It's only fitting, then, that they show up in a delicious
cobbler. Many prefer it to peach pie since there's more of the juicy
fruit involved, and it's almost always served warm. Choose very good
peaches for this dish.*

CRUST
4 cups flour
1 teaspoon salt
1 1/3 cups shortening
2/3 cup water

COBBLER
1 1/2 cups sugar
3 tablespoons flour

8 cups peaches, preferably
    fresh, peeled and sliced
1/2 cup water
1 teaspoon vanilla
1/4 cup butter, cut into chunks
1 1/2 teaspoons cinnamon
1 1/2 tablespoons sugar

Preheat oven to 400 degrees F. Grease a 13-by-9-inch baking
pan (glass preferred).

In bowl of food processor or by hand, mix flour, salt and
shortening until crumbly.

Add water, a little at a time, until dough comes together as a
pie crust dough. Do not add too much water or dough will be
sticky; dough should just hold together when pressed.

Divide dough in half and form each into a ball. Wrap one in
plastic and refrigerate.

On a floured surface, roll the other ball to 1/8 inch thickness.
Cover bottom and sides of greased baking pan.

In a large mixing bowl, combine sugar and flour; mix well.
Add peaches, water, and vanilla. Stir well. Pour mixture into
prepared crust; dot with butter chunks.

On floured surface, roll out second ball of dough to rectangle to cover baking dish. Lay dough over filling, sealing edges and crimping well. Vent by cutting X's in the pie top crust. Sprinkle crust with cinnamon and sugar.

Bake at 400 degrees F for one hour or until crust is golden and filling bubbles through crust. Remove and cool slightly before serving warm with ice cream.

Makes eight or 10 servings.

BANANAS FOSTER

*Here's another "must" when you go to New Orleans: bananas foster.
Take care when working with the alcohol; pour it into a container
before pouring into pan to ignite; a flame can travel up the liquid,
back to the bottle and explode. A long-handled lighter is a convenient
tool for this.*

4 ripe bananas, peeled, sliced
   lengthwise
4 tablespoons unsalted butter
1/2 cup dark brown sugar
1 teaspoon cinnamon
1 teaspoon freshly ground
   nutmeg

Juice of 1 lemon
2 tablespoons banana liqueur
1/2 cup brandy
1/2 cup rum
1 quart top-quality vanilla or
   dulce de leche ice cream

In a glass measuring cup, measure out brandy and rum and
set aside until needed.

In a skillet (do not use nonstick) over medium high heat, melt
butter. Add brown sugar, cinnamon and nutmeg; stir constantly
to combine. Mixture will caramelize. Add bananas and heat
through, coating with brown sugar mixture.

Remove skillet from flame, and stir in banana liqueur. Carefully add brandy-rum mixture. If mixture does not ignite
from hot butter, tilt pan and ignite with long-handled lighter
or match. (Note: Use extreme caution when doing this.) Cook
over low heat until flame dies out and alcohol is evaporated.
Add juice of lemon and swirl pan to combine.

Serve mixture hot over vanilla, or dulce de leche ice cream
in a heatproof glass bowl.

Makes four servings.

PRALINES

Visit New Orleans without tasting one of those world-famous pra-lines? Never! Can't get there? Here's the recipe. For best results, make these on a dry day; humidity can wreak havoc with the texture.

5 cups sugar
1 can (14 ounces) condensed milk
1 cup regular milk
5 cups pecans, halves or broken pieces

1 teaspoons salt
1/2 cup butter or margarine (see note)
1 tablespoon vanilla

Have ready two large baking sheets lined with parchment paper or waxed paper; set aside.

Combine sugar, condensed milk and regular milk in a large, heavy-bottomed pot or cast-iron skillet. Stir over medium heat until sugar is melted and mixture is smooth. Add pecans and stir.

Bring mixture to a boil, and cook at a low boil for 20 minutes, stirring constantly to prevent scorching. Stir in salt. Add butter, stirring until melted; add vanilla and mix well. Remove from heat, stirring well.

Caution: Take care in working with syrup as it can cause serious burns. Drop mixture by a small ladle or large serving spoon onto prepared baking sheet; mixture will spread slightly so leave room in between pralines. Stir often to keep pecan-candy mixture proportionate.

Allow to cool; remove from paper and store, with parchment paper between layers, in covered tin. Makes approximately 18 large pralines.

Note: Do not use tub margarine or spreads; the water they contain will cause this recipe to fail.

STRAWBERRY SHORTCAKE

Strawberry shortcakes are a simple and fine dessert but can look exceptionally elegant when served in pretty layers in old green Depression glass. Fresh whipped cream is a must – you wouldn't want to ruin the shortcake with anything store-bought.

5 cups sliced strawberries
1/2 cup sugar

CRUST
2 cups self-rising flour
2 tablespoons sugar

1/4 cup butter or shortening (do not use soft margarine)
3/4 cup sweet milk
1/4 cup butter, approximately, softened
Whipped cream, for serving

Put sliced berries in a medium bowl. Pour sugar over and stir lightly. Refrigerate until using.

Make shortcakes: Stir together sugar and flour. Cut cold butter or shortening into flour mixture until coarse crumbs are formed. Add milk, stirring with fork. Mixture should be doughlike.

Turn dough out onto floured surface and knead briefly. Roll to a rectangle about 1/2 inch thick. Use a rubber spatula to coat top of dough with butter. Fold dough in half. Spread more butter on dough. Fold in half again. Wrap dough in plastic and refrigerate until well chilled; at least 30 minutes

Preheat oven to 425 degrees F.

On lightly floured surface, roll out dough to rectangle shape, approximately 1/2 inch thick. Cut into 12 same-size rectangles. Place dough pieces on greased cookie sheets.

Bake at 425 degrees F for about 17 minutes or until pillowy

and golden brown. Remove and cool slightly.

To serve, place one shortcake on each plate, top with berries and their juice and repeat with second shortcake. Top with whipped cream.

Makes six servings.

WEIGHTS & MEASURES
U.S. Measures to Metric

Capacity
1 teaspoon = 5 ml
1 tablespoon = 15 ml
1 fluid oz. = 34 ml
1/2 cup = 120 ml
1 cup = 240 ml

Weight
3.5 ounces = 100 grams
1.10 pounds = 500 grams
2.205 pounds = 1 kilogram

Oven Temperature Guide

	F	C
Warm	300	150
Moderately Warm	325	160
Medium	350	180
Moderately Hot	375	190
Hot	400-415	200-210
Broil	550	288

**Consider other offerings in our line of acclaimed regional
cookbooks:** "Small size, big taste!" – *Galveston Daily News*

Salsa! Salsa! Salsa!
A handy guide to making salsas for every occasion, to grace any cuisine. "Hottest book on the shelf."
– Bud Kennedy, *Fort Worth Star-Telegram*.
ISBN 1-892588-05-6. List $5.95

Tex Mex 101
"From family favorites to gourmet creationsm recipes from Texans who know."
– *Sherman-Denison Herald News*.
ISBN 1-892588-01-3. List $5.95

Championship Chili
Winning recipes that swept top honors at the leading national cook-offs. "Best darn chili on either side of the Pecos!" – *Big Bend Sentinel*.
ISBN 1-892588-03-X. List $5.95

Louisiana's Tables: A Culinary Heritage Tour
"Makes a terrific, inexpensive choice for anyone who wants a quick reference guide to Louisiana's food." –*The Advocate*, Baton Rouge, La. Advocate. 200 pages.
ISBN 978-1-892588-586. List $7.99

A Cajun Family Cookbook
"The Lafayette native's pocket-size cookbook packs a punch with 94 pages of quick-andeasy, Louisiana-inspired dishes." – *Lafayette Advertiser*
ISBN 978-1-892588-302. List $5.95